Hanuman Chalisa

Pocket Book in English

Art by: Sujata Saha

Publisher: DivineBharat

ISBN: 978-93-343-4408-0

Website: www.divinebharat.co

For inquiries, contact:

Email: info.divinebharat@gmail.com

Content

Hanuman Chalisa

Shri Guru Charan Saroj raj
Nija manu Mukura sudhari
Baranau Raghuvar Bimal Jasu
Jo Dayaku Phala Chari
Budheeheen Tanu Jannike
Sumiro Pavan Kumara
Bal Buddhi Vidya Dehoo
Mohee Harahu Kalesh Vikaar

Jai Hanuman gyan gun sagar

Jai Kapis tihun lok ujagar

Ram doot atulit bal dhama

Anjani putra Pavan sut nama

Mahabir vikram Bajrangi

Kumati nivar sumati Ke sangi

Kanchan varan biraj subesa

Kanan Kundal Kunchit Kesha

Hath Vajra Aur Dhwaja Viraje

Kaandhe moonj janeu saaje

Sankar suvan kesri Nandan

Tej prataap maha jag vandan

Vidyavaan guni ati chatur

Ram kaj karibe ko aatur

Prabhu charitra sunibe ko rasiya

Ram Lakhan Sita man Basiya

Sukshm roop dhari Siyahi dikhava

Vikat roop dhari lank jarava

Bhim roop dhari asur sanhare

Ramachandra ke kaj sanvare

Laye Sanjivan Lakhan Jiyaye

Shri Raghuvir Harashi ur laye

Raghupati Kinhi bahut badai

Tum mama priya Bharat-hi-sam bhai

Sahas badan tumharo yash gaave
As kahi Shripati kanth lagaave
Sankadhik Brahmaadi Muneesa
Narad Sarad sahit Aheesa
Jam Kuber Dikpaal Jahan te
Kavi kobid kahi sake kahan te
Tum upkar Sugreevahin keenha
Ram milaye rajpad deenha
Tumhro mantra Vibheeshan maana
Lankeshwar Bhaye Sab jag jana
Yug sahasra yojan par Bhanu
Leelyo tahi madhur phal janu

Prabhu mudrika meli mukh mahee

Jaladhi langhi gaye achraj nahee

Durgam kaj jagat ke jete

Sugam anugraha tumhre tete

Ram duwaare tum rakhvare

Hot na agya binu paisare

Sab sukh lahai tumhari sarna

Tum rakshak kahu ko darna

Aapan tej samharo aapai

Teenon lok hank te kanpai

Bhoot pisaach Nikat nahin avai

Mahavir jab naam sunavai

Nase rog harae sab peera
Japat nirantar Hanumat beera
Sankat se Hanuman chhudavai
Man Kram Vachan dhyan jo lavai
Sab par Ram tapasvee raja
Tin ke kaj sakal Tum saja
Aur manorath jo koi lavai
Soi amit jeevan phal pavai
Charon jug partap tumhara
Hai parsiddh jagat ujiyara
Sadhu Sant ke tum Rakhware
Asur nikandan Ram dulare

Ashta siddhi nav nidhi ke data
As bar deen Janki mata
Ram rasayan tumhare pasa
Sada raho Raghupati ke dasa
Tumhare bhajan Ram ko pavai
Janam janam ke dukh bisraavai
Antkaal Raghuvar pur jayee
Jahan janam Hari Bhakt Kahayee
Aur Devta Chitt na dharahin
Hanumat sei sarv sukh karahin
Sankat kate mite sab peera
Jo sumirai Hanumat Balbeera

Jai Jai Jai Hanuman Gosain
Kripa Karahun Gurudev ki nayin
Jo shat bar path kare koi
Chhutahin bandi maha sukh hoi
Jo yeh padhe Hanuman Chalisa
Hoye siddhi saakhi Gaureesa
Tulsidas sada hari chera
Keejai Nath Hriday mahn dera

Pavan Tanay Sankat Harana
Mangala Murati Roop
Ram Lakhan Sita Sahita
Hriday Basahu Soor Bhoop

Sankat Mochan Hanuman Ashtak

Baal Samay Ravi Bhakshe Liyo Tab

Teenahun Lok Bhayo Andhiyaaron I

Taahi Son Traas Bhayo Jag Ko,

Yah Sankat Kaahu Son Jaat Na Taro

Devan Aani Karee Binatee Tab,

Chhaadee Diyo Ravi Kasht Nivaaro

Ko Nahin Jaanat Hai Jag Mein Kapi,

Sankatamochan Naam Tihaaro-2 I

Baali Kee Traas Kapees Basain Giri,

Jaat Mahaaprabhu Panth Nihaaro I

Chaunki Mahaamuni Saap Diyo Tab,

Chaahie Kaun Bichaar Bichaaro I

Kaidvij Roop Livaay Mahaaprabhu,

So Tum Daas Ke Sok Nivaaro

Ko Nahin Jaanat Hai Jag Mein Kapi,

Sankatamochan Naam Tihaaro-2I

Angad Ke Sang Len Gae Siy,

Khoj Kapees Yah Bain Uchaaro I

Jeevat Na Bachihau Ham So Ju,

Bina Sudhi Laaye Ihaan Pagu Dharo

Heree Thake Tat Sindhu Sabe Tab,

Lae Siya-Sudhi Praan Ubaaro I

Ko Nahin Jaanat Hai Jag Mein Kapi,

Sankatamochan Naam Tihaaro-2I

Raavan Traas Daee Siy Ko Sab,

Rakshasee Son Kahee Sok Nivaro

Tahi Samay Hanuman Mahaprabhu

Jae Maha Rajaneechar Maro I

Chaahat Seey Asok Son Aagi Su,

Dai Prabhumudrika Sok Nivaaro I

Ko Nahin Jaanat Hai Jag Mein Kapi,

Sankatamochan Naam Tihaaro-2I

Baan Laagyo Ur Lachhiman Ke Tab,

Praan Taje Soot Raavan Maaro I

Lai Grh Baidy Sushen Samet,

Tabai Giri Dron Su Beer Upaaro I

Aani Sajeevan Haath Die Tab,

Lachhiman Ke Tum Praan Ubaaro I

Ko Nahin Jaanat Hai Jag Mein Kapi,

Sankatamochan Naam Tihaaro-2I

Raavan Judh Ajaan Kiyo Tab,

Naag Ki Phaans Sabai Sir Daaro I

Shreeraghunaath Samet Sabai Dal,

Moh Bhayo Yah Sankat Bhaaro I

Aani Khages Tabai Hanumaan Ju,

Bandhan Kaati Sutraas Nivaaro I

Ko Nahin Jaanat Hai Jag Mein Kapi,

Sankatamochan Naam Tihaaro-2I

Bandhoo Samet Jabai Ahiraavan,

Lai Raghunaath Pataal Sidhaaro I

Debinhen Puji Bhali Vidhi Son Bali,

Deu Sabai Mili Mantr Vichaaro I

Jaaye Sahae Bhayo Tab Hee,

Ahiraavan Sainy Samet Sanhaaro I

Ko Nahin Jaanat Hai Jag Mein Kapi,

Sankatamochan Naam Tihaaro-2I

Kaaj Kiye Bad Devan Ke Tum,

Beer Mahaaprabhu Dekhi Bichaaro

Kaun So Sankat Mor Gareeb Ko,

Jo Tumase Nahin Jaat Hai Taaro I

Begi Haro Hanumaan Mahaaprabhu,

Jo Kachhu Sankat Hoe Hamaaro I

Ko Nahin Jaanat Hai Jag Mein Kapi,

Sankatamochan Naam Tihaaro-2I

Laal Deh Laalee Lase,

Aru Dhari Laal Langoor I

Vajr Deh Daanav Dalan,

Jay Jay Jay Kapi Soor

Maruti Stotra

Bheemroopi Maharudra I
Vajra Hanuman Maruti I
Vanar Anjani Suta I
Ramduta Prabhajna II 01 II

Mahabali Prandata I
Sakla Uthavi Bale I
Soukhyakari Shokharta I
Dhurta Vaishnav Gayaka II 02 II

Dinanatha Harirupa I
Sundara Jugdantara I
Pataal Devta Hanta I
Bhavya Shendurlepana II 03 II

Loknaatha Jagannatha I
Purannatha Puratana I
Punya-vanta Punya-sheela
Pavna Partoshaka II 04 II

Dvajange Uchali Baahi I
Aveshe Latla Pudhe I
Kalgri Kaalrudragi I
Dekhata Kaapti Bhaye II 05 II

Brahmaande Mael Neno I
Aavale Dantapangati I
Netrangi Chalilya Jwala I
Bhrukuti Taathilya Bale II 06 II

Puccha teh Muradele Maatha
Kerete Kundale Vari I
Suvarna Ghati Kasoti I
Ghanta Keenkini Nagara II 07 II

Thakare ParvataAisa I
Netaka Sadapatalu I
Chapalaang Pahata Moothe I
MahaViddhultePari II 08 II

Kotichya Koti Udaane I
Zhepave Uttarekade I
Mandradri-Sarikha Dronu I
Krodhi Utpatila Bale II 09 II

Aanila Maguti Nela I
Ala Gela Manogati I
Manasi Takile Mage I
Gatisi Tulna Nase II 10 II

AnuPasuni Bramhanda I
Evadha Hoot Jaatse I
BramhandaBhovti Vedhe I
VaarjPucch Ghalavu Shaake II 11 II

Tayasi Tulna Kothe I
Meeru Mandar Chakute I
Tayashi Tulna Kaisi I
Bramhandi Pahta Nase II 12 II

Araktah Dekhile Dola I
Gilile SuryaMandala I
Vaadhta Vaddhta Vaadhe I
Bhedile ShunyaMandala II 13 II

Bhooth Preeth SaamanDhadi I
Roogvyaadhi Samasthahi I
Naasti Tutati Chinta I
Annande BheemDarshane II 14 II

Hey Dhara Pandhara Shloki I
Laabhali Shoobhale Bhaali I
Drudha Deho NeeSandheHo I
Sankhya ChandraKala Kune II 15 II

Ramdasi ArrpaGanu I
KapiKulasi Maandanu I
RamRoop AntarAatma I
Darshane Doosh Naasti II 16 II

II BheemRupi Stotra Sampoorna II

Bajrang Baan

II Doha II

Nishchay prem pratith te,

binay kare sanman I

Tehi ke karaj sakal shubh,

siddha karai Hanuman II

II Chaupayee II

Jai Hanumant sant hitkari I

Suni lijai prabhu araj hamari II01II

Jan ke kaaj vilambha na kijai I

Aatur dauri maha sukha deejai II02II

Jaise kudi Sindhu wahi para I

Surasa badh paithi vistara II 03 II

Aage jayee lankini roka I

Marehu laat gaee sur loka II 04 II

Jaay Vibhishan ko sukh deenha I

Sita nirakhi param padh leenha II 05 II

Baagh ujaari Sindhu maha bora I

Ati aatur yum kaatar tora II 06 II

Akshay kumar maari sanhara I

Loom lapait Lannk ko jaara II 07 II

Laah samaan Lannk jaari gayee

Jai jai dhuni sur pur mmhah bhayee II 08 II

Ab vilaambha kehi kaaran swami I

Krupa karahu urr antaryaami II 09 II

Jai jai Lakshman praan ke daataah I

Aatur hoy dukh harahu nipaata II 10 II

Jai Giridhar jai jai sukh-sagar I

Sur samuha samartha bhatnagar II 11 II

Om Hanu Hanu Hanu Hanu Hanumant Hatile

Bairihi maru bajjrah ki kile II 12 II

Gada bajjrah lai bairihi maaro I

Maharaj prabhu daas ubaaro II 13 II

Om-kar huunkar maha-prabhu dhaavo I

Bajjra gada hanu vilambha na lavo II 14 II

Om hrim hrim hrim Hanumant Kapeesa I

Om Huum Huum Huum Hanu ari ur shisha II 15 II

Satya hou Hari shapath paay-ke I

Ram-duuth dharu maru dhaay-ke II 16 II

Jai jai jai Hanumant agaadha I

Dukkha paavat jan kehi apraadha II 17 II

Puja jap jap nem achaara I

Nahin jaanata kacchu daas tumhara II 18 II

Van upavan, mag giri gruha maahi I

Tumhare bal hum darpath nahi II 19 II

Paay paroh kar jori manavoh I

Yahi avasar abh kehi gohravoo II 20 II

Jai Anjani Kumar Balvanta I

Shankar suvan veer Hanumanta II 21 II

Badan karal kaal kul ghalak I

Ram sahay sada prati-palak II 22 II

Bhoot preth pishachya nishachar I

Agni Betal kaal mari-mar II23II

Innhe maru tohi shapath ram ki I

Rakhu naath marjaad naam ki II24II

Janaksuta Hari daas kahavoh I

Taaki shapath vilambha na lavo II25II

Jai Jai Jai dhuni hoath akasha I

Sumirath hoath dusaha dukha nasha II26II

Charan sharan kar jori manavoh I

Yahi avasar abh kehi gouravoh II 27 II

Uthu uthu chalu tohi Ram duhai I

Paayh parooh kar jori manai II 28 II

Om cha cha cha cha chapal chalanta I

Om Hanu Hanu Hanu Hanu Hanumanta II 29 II

Om han han hank deta kapi chanchal I

Om san san sahami parane khal dal II 30 II

Apne jan ko turantah ubharo I

Sumirat hoy anand hamaro II 31 II

Yaha Bajrang Baan jehi mareh I

Tahi kaho phir kaun ubareh II 32 II

Paath karai Bajrang Baan ki I

Hanumant raksha karai pran ki II 33 II

Yaha Bajrang Baan jo jaape I

Tehi te bhoot preth sabh kaape II 34 II

Dhup deyah aru jaapai hamesha I

Taake taanh nahi rahe kalesha II 35 II

II Doha II

Prem pratith-he kapi bhajai,

sada dharai urr dhyaan II

Tehi ke karaj sakala shubh,

siddha karai hanuman II

www.ingramcontent.com/pod-product-compliance
Lightning Source LLC
Chambersburg PA
CBHW042148160726
48282CB00036B/1258
* 9 7 8 9 3 3 4 3 4 4 0 8 0 *